For

D1384299

~ BEST ~
FRIENDS

By Claudine Gandolfi

Illustrated by Richard Judson Zolan

PETER PAUPER PRESS, INC.
WHITE PLAINS, NEW YORK

To the best friends anyone could wish for.
We've laughed, we've cried, then we've
laughed at what we cried about.
You know who you are.

≈

Artist: Richard Judson Zolan
Illustrations copyright ©1998
Art Licensing Properties, LLC.

Book design by Mullen & Katz

Text copyright © 1998
Peter Pauper Press, Inc.
202 Mamaroneck Avenue
White Plains, NY 10601
ISBN 0-88088-871-7
Printed in Singapore
7 6 5 4 3 2

Introduction

———— ∾ ————

One of the most precious gifts you can give yourself is a best friend. You'll know her by the way she helps you through rough times, always keeps an open mind, and enhances enjoyment of the good times. She can tell how you're feeling with just a glance or by the tone of your voice. She'll give you wings to fly and a hand to fall back on.

Let her know just how much you appreciate her. Give her a call, a visit, or a hug. If you're searching for just the right thing to say, the following pages may offer some inspiration.

C. G.

*L*ife is a symphony and
friendship is its theme.

❧

*B*e the best friend you can be and
you'll have the best friends that
you could ever want.

Best Friends

Lend an ear to someone who needs it.
In return, not only will you receive
a shoulder to cry on but a friend
to share good times with.

～

A best friend is the sister
that destiny forgot to give you.

When you can
both laugh at
past indiscretions,
you know you share an
unbreakable bond.

Best Friends

A best friend will
congratulate you on a job well done and
console you when you need it.

~

*Y*our best friend,
like your conscience, will always guide
you to the right decision.

Old friends are like your favorite
sweater—sensible, warm, and forgiving.

~

Distance and time
cannot alter a friendship.

Best Friends

Like classic works of art, once
thought lost, friendships become more
dear when rediscovered.

Take the time to contact an old friend;
you'll be surprised at how quickly
you return to your old banter.

Best Friends

Laughter, tears, joys, and fears—a
friend makes each more special.

~

Everyone has a "best friend"
during each stage of life.
Only a precious few
have the same one.

A friend
will never
judge you,
only your
actions.

Best Friends

You can tell you've been friends a
long time when your friend can finish
your sentences for you.

Like the stars, friends sparkle and
shine when the night seems darkest.

Best Friends

Sometimes your friend isn't of the
same mind as you, but you're always
of the same spirit.

Laugh and the world laughs with you,
cry and your friend will too.

Best Friends

Some friendships are forged of iron,
some of gossamer, and all are
equally precious.

~

If you believe that you are the
"better friend," examine who
made you so.

Best Friends

Never pass up a chance at friendship;
it might not be offered again.

❧

Your best friend knows you
well enough to know when you
need comforting and when
you need solitude.

*F*riendship is the music of life.

∾

*Y*our best friend is a living keepsake
of all your precious moments.

No one
ever faulted a friend
for keeping
in touch.

*A*cceptance, forgiveness, and
companionship are the recipe for
a lasting friendship.

*M*emories bind friends together.

The eternal is reflected in
the laughter of friends.

As you grow older you tend to
remember more of the joys of friendship
and fewer of the quarrels.

*Y*our best friend can be more
forgiving of your faults than you are.

*F*riends get excited when you have
news that you're dying to share.

Best Friends

Guard your friendships with
great care; they are some of
your most valuable possessions.

~

Like snowflakes, each friend is
a precious gift.
No two are exactly alike.

$\mathcal{T}$hough you are
not the same as you were
when you first became friends,
neither is your friendship.
It has mellowed and
become more valuable.

Best Friends

Sometimes the melodies of friendship
may differ, but it's the harmony that
makes life sweet.

Your best friend is the
one perfect rose in a large and lovely
bouquet of acquaintances.

Best Friends

A friend's smile is like a beacon
welcoming you home.

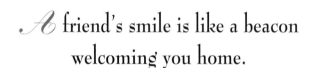

Trust is a fragile part of friendship;
it must be earned and should
never be broken.

During your most trying times,
you don't need to see your friend to
know that she is there for you.

~

In giving of yourself you receive
the gift of friendship.

*S*haring memories
with friends is like
reading a classic.
It's always enjoyable
to go back and re-read
the best parts.

*L*aughter accompanies friendship
as dance does music.

*E*mbrace your friends as you do life—
with ardor and with care.

Best Friends

*N*ever withhold friendship from
your friend; it may cost you more
than you think.

~

*Y*our best friend has seen your
true self, warts and all, and still
values your friendship.

Very rarely will a heart-to-heart
with a dear friend fail to
make things seem better.

Sometimes a friend made under the
most unusual of circumstances can
become the most treasured.

Like flowers, the best friendships
retain their beauty and perfume after
the bloom has faded.
They are everlastings.

～

Best friends have mastered the art of
hearing, not just empty listening.

A friendship
that has weathered
all kinds of problems
will grow stronger
for doing so.

*F*riends are viewed not just through
the act of seeing, but through a loving
heart and a forgiving spirit.

~

*W*elcome friendship with a warm
embrace and give it with full abandon.

If you willingly give advice to a friend,
do not be reluctant to accept advice as well.

~

A comfortable silence between friends
speaks volumes.

If laughter and forgiveness are the blocks that build a friendship, loyalty is the mortar that keeps it in place.

~

A best friend never expects a favor for each favor given.

A friend
will not only let you
laugh at her
expense—she'll
join in.

Best Friends

In the eyes of a friend your
true self is reflected.

~

Even during the winter of life an old
friend brings a spring to your step.

Friends

are

life's dessert.